Purity of Absence

Purity of Absence

poems by

Dave Margoshes

Porcepic Books
an imprint of

Beach Holme Publishing
Vancouver

First Edition

This book is published by Beach Holme Publishing, 226-2040 West 12th Avenue, Vancouver, B.C. V6J 2G2. *www.beachholme.bc.ca.* This is a Porcepic Book.

The publisher gratefully acknowledges the financial support of the Canada Council for the Arts and of the British Columbia Arts Council. The publisher also acknowledges the financial assistance received from the Government of Canada through the Book Publishing Industry Development Program (BPIDP) for its publishing activities.

Editor: Michael Carroll
Production and Design: Jen Hamilton
Cover Art: *Red Hue Moon* by Christine Lynn, acrylic on canvas, copyright © 2000. Licence granted by Canadian Artists Representation Copyright Collective.
Author Photograph: Myek O'Shea

Printed and bound in Canada by Marc Veilleux Imprimeur

National Library of Canada Cataloguing in Publication Data

Margoshes, Dave, 1941-
Purity of absence

Poems.
"A Porcepic book."
ISBN 0-88878-419-8

I. Title.
PS8576.A647P87 2001 C811'.54 C2001-910123-6
PR9199.3.M354P87 2001

For Ilya, as always

Contents

The Marriage Bed 27

The Satisfaction of Knowing 57

Acknowledgements

Many of the poems in this collection have appeared, often in earlier versions, in the following magazines and anthologies: *Ariel*, *Border Crossings*, *Canadian Forum*, *Canadian Literature*, *CV2*, *Cross-Canada Writers Quarterly*, *Dalhousie Review*, *Dandelion*, *diverge*, *Fiddlehead*, *Grain*, League of Canadian Poets' *Museletter*, *NeWest Review*, *Poetry Canada Review*, *Pottersfield Portfolio*, *Prairie Fire*, *Queen's Quarterly*, *Textual Studies in Canada*, *This Magazine*, *Towards 2000* (Fifth House Publishers), *Vallum*, *Vintage 1991* (Sono Nis Press), and *Windsor Review*.

Some poems were broadcast on the CBC programs *Ambience* and *Gallery*.

"The Persistent Suitor" won the Stephen Leacock Poetry Award from the Orillia International Poetry Festival in 1996. "On the Beach" won second prize in the 1997 Saltwater Poetry Contest. "Dec. 6, Montreal" won second prize in the League of Canadian Poets' 1991 National Poetry Contest.

My thanks to the editors, producers, and judges.

Thanks also to the Saskatchewan Writers Guild's colony committee, which operates writers and artists colonies at Emma Lake and St. Peter's Abbey, Muenster, Saskatchewan, where many of these poems were written.

And especial thanks to Christine Lynn for *Red Hue Moon,* the painting on the cover.

And more thanks to George Amabile, whose lines "the purity of absence/kindles appetites that hiss/and fuse. One/last beginning," from his poem "Tangents and Vectors," are used, with permission, as an epigraph for my poem "Purity of Absence." I heard George read his poem at Heaven bookshop in Winnipeg in spring 1996 and, struck by that phrase "the purity of absence," immediately began my poem on the back of a napkin.

God’s Tears

The Perfect Moment

for Shaya

The farther you go
the closer you come
to every thing
you always thought
was out of your reach,
the perfect breathless moment
crystallizing,
evaporating.

This is the way
the world turns
itself inside out
of the way
beyond anything
you could imagine

the rising star
shaking off night
into the mouth
of a jealous sun

the rising star
casting its light
into the shining
eyes of the beholder

your light
illuminating something
we've never seen before.

Strikes Often

> Men are struck by lightning five times as often as women.
>
> —Newspaper Item

Taller, of course,
more foolhardy, more's
the fool, and more likely
to have forgotten an umbrella,
to be out walking and fail to notice
rain assailing our unprotected lives
the way your love can if we
let it, but that alone can't explain
why our lives are in jeopardy,
why we take the chances no one
would reasonably assume we
should, not in this life
with all its teeth and broken glass.

Montreal haunts us the way livers
do drunks. Sick and complaining,
they insist we somehow are at fault,
we who take all the chances,
who put ourselves ahead
of whatever comes, that we brought
it on ourselves, and maybe we did.
Say something often enough
and even the liar starts to believe
it, let alone the altar boys,
lip-syncing the litany, *big boys*
don't cry, rats' tails and snails,
that's what boys are made of.

When it does strike, lightning,
it doesn't do it twice but over
and over again till we've got
the drill in our sleep, dreams

blossoming up like fish surfacing
with bubbles for kisses, till
the choices dry up, even the few
we started with. The house
is in darkness, the children
asleep, your breath steady as tide
on the pillow, the owl silent
in its tree. We lie awake,
listening for thunder.

Eat Their Own

> Biologists have found that more than 1,300 species of animals will make meals of their own families.
>
> —Newspaper Item

Deepest night and the growls
you wake to are of the belly
not the throat, that ache
ripples from the gut rather
than from that mythical heart
the songwriters celebrate,
muscle pulsating, waiting
to be fed.
Heartburn is a condition
of digestion, not emotion.

Still, the temptation
to spin on spine's axis
to your partner defenceless
in sleep is strong, nibbling
at lips that cannot protest,
gorging yourself on willing flesh,
blind mother turning in the nest
driven by something deeper
than hunger, devouring
placentas of love.

The Cruel Air

Under a tree, I sit
growing roots, listening
to the immense noise, opening
my eyes to light
without end.
The sun splinters, a narrow
man comes down
the road, stops
to listen, then lopes
the dusty way he's come.
The road is empty, the sky
a hole letting in
the promised menace.

The iron ring of his foot
on the cobblestones, a circle
in a pool of water. *I wanted*
to be a good man
he cried as he fell
but only the air
heard, the thin cruel air.
So quickly then
this eggshell
shatters. But what
shall we do
with this dark?

4H

after the fair
we took down the tents
wiped the cotton candy
from our feet
and washed our hands
in a stream of water
from a cold iron pipe
the livestock had kissed.

the sun was going down
and the children were gone
leaving deflated snowmen
of torn tickets
and apple sticks
in the swamp
where the midway had raged.

we walked hand in hand
the wind rippling soft
at the ribbons on our breasts
swirling the eddies of gold
left behind by judges
who should have known better
having known us so long.

well there's always next year
and the years after that
rolling like meadows
across the horizon
to bring down the sky
and it's not the winning
that matters
but the way we die.

Balancing Act

for Mickey

balancing on the high
wire, your parents' world
dizzy at your feet, ants
in a cage charlie chaplining
below, you feel your stomach
blossom against your heart,
your heart itself soaring
through air without benefit
of a net, your eyes blurred
not from tears but the speed
of your blood finding its own
balance, its own
way

jumping *off* the high wire
you find yourself falling
deliriously
into yourself

Mullin's

If Mullin's Hardware is really
the centre of the city
as the old-timers say, forget
the maps, the city plan,
then what of the Centre
of the Arts, Queensbury Downs,
what about Market Square?
They're deserted tonight, empty
as the shells of gypsy moths, their
eyes alight with visions of the city
trembling in their wake, a naked
city, its bum bare as the day
it was born.

Tonight, the city's pulse runs
ragged along 13th, a red current
of light leading—where else?—but
to Mullin's, not just the centre
of the city but the universe,
to hell with the maps
and compasses, to Mullin's,
where a woman in a red bandanna
is dancing alone in the shadow
of the cathedral, its hands thrown up
in joy, her eyes filled with light
reflected from the sputtering streetlamp,
her feet just barely touching
the ground. You and I
are getting to know each other
in ways they haven't dreamed of
at the track or the Superstore,
in ways explained for a dime
in the hardware, third aisle
at the end.

DST

buddy, back east
time goes back
and there ain't no way
to stop it

out here
time matters more
due to the growing
and shape of things

take the time
yourself
to think it over
and come around

life goes on
the way it will
and that's fact,
like rain falls *down*

behind the times
lies the land:
keeping count
refusing to lie

Little Caesar on TV

Mother of mercy
is this the end of Rico?
Or does the pulse of desire
that lifted him up keep racing
through rain-slick streets
like a speeding roadster,
the fates on its tail in hot pursuit.
Flaherty, you bastard,
how easy it is for you to sneer
at ambition extinguished,
you whose only hopes revolve
around slipping the cuffs
on wrists of men with clearer sight,
squeezing the juice from fingers
that have moulded life in all
its uncertainty and rigour,
that have taken chances.

He wound up in the gutter
that he came from, just as you told
the scribblers he would, just
the way your divine plan dictated
he should, but not because
of any blur in his vision,
any failing of his stout heart—
the way you would have had it—
but because of the fundamental
flaw in his logic: sure, be big,
the heavens are vast, stars beyond
counting and man is puny unless
he dares to stand on tiptoe
and push his hand beyond his reach.
Sure, Rico, be a big shot,

the way the egg stains on your plate
predict, but don't you dare
spit on the dance,
or step on the toes of the dancer.

Deadman's Eyes

for Charlie Niehuis

Luis José Mongi, last man executed
in the United States before the high court
blew the whistle, gassed June 27, 1967,
in Canon City, willed his corneas
to two convicts, one at Buena Vista,
the other to Rick Gardner, hospital orderly
at Canon who'd done him kindnesses,
a trustee who'd embezzled clinic funds,
hands shaking with blindness closing in
the way death sniffed around at José's heels,
"I won't need them anymore," he told
the warden, Big Jim Patterson, who
would pull the switch hissing in the gas,
flip to the end. He'd beaten his
common-law wife to death with his hands.

Patterson took sick, wound up
in hospital, and called for Gardner
to be brought from the pen to look
after him, doze in a hard-backed chair
beside the bed through the night
when ghosts of José and other spirits
came back to dance their death jigs
around him, the twitches of gas
rushing through blood to claim it,
José's eye in Rick's head gazing
through the night at Patterson's face
without rancour, without compassion
but with calm.

Upright

Lewis Carroll, the author of *Alice in Wonderland,* wrote standing up.
—Newspaper Item

Not upright but upstanding,
seeking not after flesh
of young girls but spirit,
his eyes on the heaven above
them rather than within.

This agony he feels,
a love as yet unarticulated,
forced into metaphor the way
icing sugar takes on another life
as the sure hand of the baker
squeezes it through mortar and tube
into hearts and bows, a daintiness
beyond the ken of mere romance,
this agony penetrating to the root
of teeth, rotting the bone.

Standing, yes, of course,
and on tiptoes, the posture
not only of poets but of poetry
itself, standing, all the better to see
the angle of sun
arcing the horizon,
all the closer
to the length of our reach.

Game 6, World Series, Bottom of the 10th, 2 Outs

Those hands
have been very important
for 24 victories this season
        and *very* important
for seven innings of this game
but now all Roger Clemens can do
is fold them and watch.

Thanks for the poetry, Joe,
but the sentiment stinks.
Carter doubles
and Knight singles,
sending him to third
and redeeming himself
for that error in the seventh—
        redemption, Joe, that's the angle—
and Carter scores when a wild pitch
sends Gedman scrambling
and Mookie hits this sputtering grounder
down the first-base line,
an easy out, except something—
God, maybe, that's what Knight says—
makes Buckner daydream it out
of his glove, spins around to watch it go
with the helplessness of a bartender
feeling the Scotch splash out
of the glass and onto his best shirt—
all this because we don't quit,
Mookie says in the postgame interview,
we never say die,
and some things are certain
despite the combined wisdom
of the colourmen,
        even you, Vin:

as the ball is thrown
so shall it be caught,
and something—maybe it was God
but maybe it was just Carter—
says no, damn it, and no force
on earth can stop
the ball's spin when it hits
a fault in ground no one
could have known was there.

Changed Title

> The painting *Whistler's Mother* was originally called *Arrangement in Grey and Black Number One.*
>
> —Newspaper Item

Only a woman, a mother,
neither substance nor form
with the force or weight
of triangle and square
to anchor it to canvas and mind,
merely flesh, lacking
the permanence of parchment.

Yet surely there is
something
of interest in this
arrangement of colour and form
beyond the obvious bow
to the sentiment, the tug
at the romantic forelock.

She sits in an arrangement
of bone and flesh that defies
the contortionist's logic,
her lips composed in
a smile smeared with sex
beyond flesh and nerve, beyond
gender to the root of biology.

She has just said something,
waits listening for answers.
Her heart beats, blood flows,
the *smell* of her lifts itself
off the canvas the way a fighter
must before the bell, raising his head
the way she does hers, into perfection.

Seeing the Future

Late April mornings, when so much
and so little push at the edge
of sleep, tearing us away
from sweet oblivion,

applesauce life slides around,
filling us with warm expectation,
a bath deep as oceans
but shallow

as our breath as we stir
in dream waiting to enfold
us, take us under
far as the curve of sky.

This is the future, with past
and present spun around
like tinselled gift wrap
to make the package alluring

despite the hollow box
it hides, the stink of rotting
grass, the ache in the back
of the mouth. This

is the future, the face
staring back, the voice
at the other end, the touch
in the night, the road

on the other side
of the folded map leading
nowhere, circling back
to where we started,

April morning, sleep.

Forked Tongues

for Paulette Dubé

Your tongue is
split, a shell
cloven in two

one ribbon of flesh
rabbiting across prairie
where the enormity of sky
squeezes you small, the other
curling through mountain
passes where you grow
into yourself, a nautilus

one tongue bitten sore
with accent, its mate licked
smooth, one dark as the wing
of a heron glimpsed
overhead, the other bright
as the eyes
of the silver fish
it swoops down on.

Your tongue is
split, a leaf torn
along the stem

the poem it sings
a metaphor
for the desire
pulling you, pushing
you, pressing you
down, hurling you into air
bereft of meaning.

Your tongue is
split, your heart
whole.

The Persistent Suitor

Three days into the treatment,
the chemical teeth gnawing
their way through her veins,
Yvonne passes a bad night,
wrestling with Death, who slips
not *under* her bed as the demons
she feared as a child liked to do
but *into* it, cozying right up
beside her, cuddling, hands all over her
breasts and backside, foul breath
singeing the tender flesh below her
earlobes, hardly a gentleman,
she thinks, remembering
the Emily Dickinson poem she read
in university, no, more like
the boys she'd fended off that same year,
all intellect and hands but more
of the latter, she and her roommate
would laugh, but, just the same, nothing
to be afraid of,
and not now, either, despite
that stinging breath, the clawing
hands, the persistent
fingers, no, the old defence
still works, the defence
of last resort her mother taught her,
a knee,
doubled up quickly, where it hurts
the most, even for Death, not so
proud now, not
so fearsome. But this is
just the fourth morning, days
before her hair turns white, before
her stomach turns itself inside
out, days before the first bouquet
of his roses arrives.

Pride of Flesh

for Melanie

Pride of flesh, skin's vanity,
blood's boast, hubris of bone,
these are gifts we bring
to this arrangement, virtues
we have more than enough of.

In the mirror, my image wrestles
yours to the glass, distorting
not just what we see but the sense
we have when gazing at perfection
of being close to what god whispered,

to what he may have had in store
for Eve and Adam had they not been
fools and thrown away heaven
just for the dubious pleasures
of sex and knowledge. For so little,

they quit the garden, crossing
a boundary beyond which
there is no conception, brave
Columbuses sticking out their tongues
at earth's edge, leaving god's forgiveness

behind them in the constant slant of sky.
How right the bard was, what fools
these mortals be, all the more so
if they think they aren't. Fools
who gaze at themselves with wonder,

with reverence, as if seeing something
more than what god had intended,
the simple arrangement of his form,
there on the glass, the reflection
burned with balm onto our perfect eyes.

Eat Book

for Salman Rushdie

> Ernest Toller, an antifascist German author and playwright, was arrested in 1933 by the Nazis and forced to eat one of his books.
>
> —Newspaper Item

Eating our words, we find
ourselves face-to-face
with realities we could only
guess at before, the bitter
taste of metaphor staining
our tongues like blood ballooning
aortas into comic-book dialogue
bereft of all distinctions.

There is nourishment
to be gained from narrative
and simile, from truth spread
thin as peanut butter all the more
palatable, sticking to mouth's
wonder-struck roof, embedding itself
between the teeth of lies, annoyingly
beyond tongue's tangled reach

but things we need to say
catch in our own teeth
if we hold them in too long
disallowing the natural propensity
of nature to seek its own level
abhorring vacuums sucked from our guts
by words sharp as bayonets, the turning
away of each tiny, perfect ear.

Perseid

Sage Hill, Saskatchewan, August 1993

Backs turned to artificial light,
we marched up the hill like soldiers
to battle, laughing to give
ourselves courage, our faces
lifted to the trembling sky, god's
ruffled breast opening to enclose
us, twenty poets or more ranged along
the curving road to the exposed bones
of the radar station, its voice
stilled, its ear no longer cocked
to heaven. We would be radar,
hurling our pulse into darkness
in hopes of making contact,
some message with clues to god's
devious plan. We lay on gravel,
the whole black bowl of heaven
curving above us, its glittering
teeth, ursa major, aurora
grinning their secrets the way
they always do, cold, implacable,
and tears, god's tears
shedding their silent path
into our own, arrows of light
piercing our open hearts
with their silence, flash
and glitter, the meaning
escaping us. Later, in our beds
we felt the gravel encoded
on our shoulder blades, closed
our eyes to the brilliant sky
repeating itself behind
our lids, ursa major,
aurora borealis,
and tears,
god's tears.

The Marriage Bed

The Sound of My Voice

The sound of my voice
tearing the unyielding air
startles me as much
as it does you,
the loudness a slap in my own
face as much as in yours,
so much of a surprise that
I flinch, the look in your eye
a mirror image of that in my own.

It fills the quaking room, bees
swarming not around honey
but blood, the blood rising
in your scalp, hair standing
end on end, my love a dead bee
in your hand, that suspect
suddenly, that filled with harm,
that much something you didn't think
you'd see again.

Voice, though, is mechanics,
thrumming of air over chords
laid down like utility lines
deep in the throat beyond sight
and turning back; words code
waiting to be broken, careless
stones without weight
of their own beyond that
which cannot be taken back.

The sound of my voice echoes,
my *own* voice that seems
to come from someone else,
the ventriloquist inside me
I have to face, the white heat

of anger turning to snow,
melting, my voice incomplete
without answer, yours, two voices
finally, healing the silence.

Silver Anniversary

for Ilya

It takes a long time
for the heart to catch up
with the senses,
for what the eyes
see to filter through
the ganglia of nerves
reaching like spider breath
past the mind to the quick
of feeling, beyond
blood's mere thrill
at the abrasion of flesh
on fingers insinuating its way
through pores like god tiptoeing
across heaven, careful not
to wake the angels.

All that takes
an endless time, we know, but
how long does it take
for the senses to catch up
with the heart? Is it
measured in moments
or years, love letters
or calendars of lifetimes,
their pages tangled in wind
the way your hair gets
in summer when you allow
it to grow, reaching for sky?
These are questions
only lovers would bother
to ask, expecting no more
answer than consolation.

Anniversaries are squares
on calendar pages crossed
off each year like water
over a dam, one, two, ten times,
twenty-five, green stones
without name precious as jade,
each year precious as the one
before, stones precious as silver,
silver precious as gold,
water precious as blood,
blood flowing separately within
each of us, keeping us
separate, out of the reach
of romance and the terrible
impulse to join. But
blood is glue as well as solvent,
pasting calendar pages
into sheaves of years enduring
as spines of handmade books,
books of leather centuries old,
pages of parchment, pages on which
is written one story in two hands,
ink precious as blood,
the words its script spiders
across the pages indecipherable
to any interpretation
but the heart's, a secret
to everything but the senses.

By Canoe to Loon Lake

Your skin numbs
with electric currents
of desire to sheath
this body in sieved light
of pure energy, push
the heart and other organs
this way and that, squeeze
the bones into puzzles
of tangled chrome, entrails
pointing the way
to a future already
imagined, not yet
grasped.

But evenings, you slide
into glassy waters of sound
winding around the loon's
bright pulsing throat, raindrops
thrumming darkness, air
sucked in on itself in whoops
of shivering pleasure, songbirds
dense as Christmas shoppers
in verdant desire, preening
the way you never could have,
opening something. Your hand
closes, opens, breath rattles
your throat into looping dream,
our love a loon, seeing in the dark,
circling you, feathering you down.

Going South for the Winter

Going south for the winter
the car broke down and you
had to stand shivering
at the bus stop, arrive
at the new place like a tourist,
suitcase in damaged hand, this
silly grin on your face where
there should have been pain. Well,
a new decade, with the end
of a millennium stamping its feet
in the hall, deserves as much, even
when you are on a budget.

All the time,
the weather pressing in,
its rattling breath giving
face to the splintering glass,
stray cat shoulder to the door
insistent as frigid daylight
after night's long warm hollow tongue,
cold bugs swarming in exquisite symmetry
of pain and pleasure, tree-bark skin
crackling, its howls
filling the celadon air.

How would it be possible
to survive another winter,
another year not only in the life
of the dwindling planet but in your
own life, not yet at the same critical
mass? But going south is more
than realignment in terms of direction,
more than geography, going south
is a turning into yourself, where fire

continues to burn, not damnable fire
but the pure flame of chemistry, transforming
one thing into another.

Thirty-Five Below

Thirty-five below, forty-five above
the span between temperature
and age is more than one
of degree, mere number, adding
up as they do to the sum
of this season of your disenchantment.
Little things prickle: aching
hands, the dog's barking splinters
of ice tearing at night's thin
cloth, the barometer
of your father's pulse, the job
a dull toothache always beyond reach
at the back of the jaw, allergies
swimming out of sight, aching
knees, for god's sake.

Still, there are solaces
and consolations. One foot
after another in patterns
dancers and walkers weave
through combination locks
of rhythm and time, splitting
open heart's crinkly cellophane,
porcelain trees blinkering
the path between house and garage
where birds rule the wingless beasts
below, spring buried in rotting
snow a bomb waiting to take
root, explode among the rhubarbs,
my love a chinook
sighing on your neck.

The Door

Behind a door
the ticking of a clock
muffled by cotton batting,
rain on a tarpaper roof
through the wool of sleep,
the beating of a heart,
murmuring in protest,
that softly, that much danger,
that much promise.

The door slams closed
not at your choosing
but at the mercy of wind
coiled at your side, stinging
the foot you've wedged along
the jamb, dust springing around
the shape of absence you leave
behind, surprising the blood
into your face, spilling over.

The door is an idea
taking shape behind itself
in narrowing light. The closing
is an idea of darkness, the opening
an idea illuminating the passage
through which you move, finding
your certain way. The door
creaks, resisting. Together,
we lean the irresistible weight

of love against it.

Taking Heart

Taking heart comes
harder these windchill days
when war and lunatics
crow over the front pages

and, breakfast done,
my morning routine
swallows the careless idle
like gaping washing machines

spitting us out damp
and wrinkled by noon,
ready for ironing, folding,
the endless putting away.

But by the time
the afternoon bites in
and begins to swing
its shadowy leg over

the fence and darkness
sidles up to tap
at the window,
the chill inside fades

and I can hear
the click of heels
wooing me; the dog
perks up her head,

creature of habit,
in recognition.
The snap of lock,
the door's creaky swing

takes me by surprise
over again, each time,
even though I know
your signals by heart.

There is a moment
then when I awaken
for the first time
really of the day

and like linen starched,
folded in your arms,
I do take heart
and you take mine.

Smoke

smoke
shooting straight up to god's eye
from parched mouths of his creatures

masking sky in grey like winter underwear
hung out to freeze on March's line

pulling down April's last breath,
grains of sand caught in your teeth,
rolling under the tongue to tell about pain—

giving this up is nothing compared
to putting the last match to our greater need:

imagine me without you,
the sky without light,
day without end where peace folds in
like clouds in water,
this day without love.

Learning to Breathe

Learning to run is
learning to see,
the stride encompassing
parameters of sight
beyond which there is
no conception, some brave
Franklin blinking his eyes
at the arctic glare,
god's grudging forgiveness
left behind in an inner passage
of his own making.

Learning to walk is
learning to hear,
the eloquent ear deciphering
messages tattooed on the bottom
not of your feet but your fingertips,
reaching beyond the thrust
and momentum of body
to seize the shape of yourself
in the sound of another.

Learning to love is
learning to breathe,
your own eye gauging dimensions
of your reach, the distance
between polarities, the time
it would take to cross divisions
without all the hopes
we wouldn't have dared develop
for ourselves, on our own.

Breaking the Silence

Silence like a jellyfish
blossoms beneath the surface,
gorging itself on words, what
I say, what you say, the unspoken
words that sink gently
through the sieving light
to the sea's undisturbed bottom
before they're sucked up—all
mouth and stomach, invisible
by day, transparent, ghostly
contours of its gassy shape vivid
only after dark, in the beam
of light we hold to it,
hands shaking.

Floating in that silence,
the translucent lustre
of its enforced surface
pressing down on us, soaking
up our rattly breath, we run
the risk of drowning, love
turned to bait, schools
of grinning piranha turning
our flesh to unfulfilled
promise, bones to direction signs
pointing nowhere.

The derelict sky beats down
oblivious, static hiss of surf
rising to a din, the profound
noise roiling within the heart
calling out, a muffled bell
tolling across distance too far
for lovers to swim, their arms
leaden at their sides, exhausted

by the moon, its fluted path
reading our future. Within
this mute cacophony, love
lifts its head, listens—
me calling you, you calling me—
takes up the cry.

The Marriage Bed

Getting into bed at two in the morning
the heat from the electric blanket
engulfs me, pulls me to you, the skin
on your bare hip nubbed
with dampness where the nightgown
has twisted away, a strand
of hair fine as filigreed silver
across your forehead in the pale light
from the neighbour's kitchen window.

In sleep you are always still
the girl I first came to all those years
ago, your porcelain skin tight
as the casing enfolding a rose
before it blossoms, I am that boy
who worshipped at the light radiating
from you, at your heat, the breath
stuttering through my ribs, we are
ghosts of ourselves, haunting
our present selves who cannot sleep.

In the tropical cave of our bed
we are the animals we deny being
in the fearsome clarity of day,
our clothes a disguise fooling even
ourselves, small, sleekly furred animals
chattering with fear and pleasure
as the planet spins, the tides recede,
our blood dances to venerable rhythms,
feral beasts clinging to each other
in the deep well of night,
the same love that pulls us
apart drawing us together.

Saskatoons

you come
through
the door
your pale hand
bloodied
with a slice
of pie
an offering
and I feel
my anger
crack open
the kernel
at its heart
fall
shards
of shell
littering
the floor
over which
you step
into
my arms

we hold
each other
carefully
mindful
of the teeth
below

Uncharted

Columbus stumbled
on land he thought
was India; only later
did history claim
he discovered
something unimagined
some thing he
couldn't have known;
now we know
his only discovery
was ashes, tears,
blood.

You and I stumbled
on each other,
thinking we'd discovered
another country
of the heart, a place
where we could lose
ourselves, a refuge
on the run. Our love
stumbled, found
its footing unexpectedly,
found its way
in maps it couldn't
comprehend. Only now
do we find we've
discovered something
about ourselves,
some thing we
couldn't have
imagined, the farthest
reaches of love;

brave explorers,
still searching
flat worlds
for roundness.

Anatomy

The ribs,
prayers of bone
too fragile to utter

the lungs,
waterfalls of desire
slanting toward light

the heart,
a small green stone
still winking

its tarnish of flesh
worn thin by light, by love,
its force undiminished.

The accretion of years,
the fragrant moss circling
our heads ungathered

the singing of birds
in their naked tree,
hands, lips, an open eye

the polished angle of your arm,
the fragile trap behind
the trick curve of your knee

all the bodily parts,
their sums multiplying,
the green heart blinking, blinking

as if in code.

Snow

Fifty words for snow
  a word for fresh snow
  a word for snow brittle
      as the heart's edge when it cracks
  a word for snow trampled underfoot
  one for yellow snow
  for grey snow, black snow
  one for snow glazed over with tears
  a word for snow falling like tears
  a word for snow hard as turning away
  one for melting snow, snow softened
      by a glance
  many others, too numerous to cite
  words formed by a need to express
      the inexpressible

Fifty words for love
  each one of them
  pronounced with your name

The Waking

one morning—
it may have been in
April, perhaps November—
we found we no longer were
the people we'd started
out to be

your hand
at the window
traced circles in the frost
until the world revealed
itself to us, naked
as we'd been

the bird
tangled in blue branches
ruffled its feathers
in your throat, singing
something we only half
remembered

and the dream
of a shape we might
still take shone
in the translucent sky, a dream
to be had
for the waking

Okanagan

Will spring never
arrive this year?
Already our day
and bloodless snow is spitting
spitefully through air
frigid as a long-distance call,
the sky's lungs
congested with phlegm
as yours were, a long
pneumonia ago.

Across the mountains
though the snow is thick
and pink as tapioca
beneath cherry trees
we would climb,
their hands raised
to the heavens with
surprise and joy. O
kanagan, its heart
is breaking
with the aching wait,
its arms trembling
to be filled with you,
the way mine are,
spring, winter, summer, fall

Distances

Five hundred miles, a line straight
as spider's thread across the folded map
of the country we made ours, the country
that made us in exchange
in its own image. Eight hours
by bus, the sky a swirling wheel
of stars above, an electric arrow
in the heart by phone, my finger
tracing the one clear line, the life line
on a palm, the line the cord in your neck
articulates in its stretch from head
to body, heart to tongue, inspiration
to intent to conclusion. Fifty billion
stars in the Milky Way, fifty billion
galaxies in the universe, the Hubble
hard on their tails, drawing a line
between heaven and the eye
of the astronomer, his feet
rooted to ground, his cloistered heart
thumping in his chest, fifty billion
stars, five hundred
miles, your hand,
mine, so far, so close

Purity of Absence

> The purity of absence
> kindles appetites that hiss
> and fuse. One
> last beginning.
>
> —George Amabile, "Tangents and Vectors"

Absence makes the heart
grow not fonder necessarily
but fuller, pails overflowing
with melt as you bail
the window wells at the close
of the longest winter, its cold
still lingering in the hills
like snipers protecting the flanks
of a retreating army. Why *was*
the winter so cold, so long?
The shape of your absence
in my bed, at the table, the feel
of your absence in my arms
at dusk, the absence of your voice
murmuring good-night, its silence
resonating, the absence
of your scent on the pillow, your
absence carved in ice, traced
with a finger in the frost
on a window, the purity
of absence, the hard, brilliant seed
at its core, and finally the arrival
of its end, my mouth filling
with water, our hearts
filling with melted snow
beginning the long hiss
to boil, the pot spilling over

A New Nightgown

A new nightgown arrives
in the mail, blue as a bruise
just starting to darken, cotton
soft as bandage, your skin
puckering with itch
at the hint of anything less
or more. Long skirt, long
sleeves, high collar, and how
I envy it, how deep in the night
it will hold you in its arms.

The Recorder

You put the polished wood to your lips,
where mine have been, whispering secrets
even I don't know, secrets of sound
and breath and the longing that rises
from deep in the bellows of the heart.

One note, a second, a third stutter
through the cloistered air like lovers
dumbstruck by foolish luck, then find
their footing, orchestrate themselves
into a panoply of shimmering sound.

The dog gives me a baleful look
as we retreat, leaving you propped
on the bed, all your attention turned
to the magic wand in your hands.
One wave, and all your bidding may be done.

Music rises, maddening the air
with its insistence, the pure glacial pane
of transparency through which only you
can see the shape of its conclusion emerge.
Outside the door, I stand, listening,

gathering notes like love in my arms.

A Bird in the House

How quickly the house fills
with music, the anorexic notes
turning the dog into a critic, head
cocked with wonder as she urges
them to *eat*, put flesh on the bones
she would gladly chew. The polished
maple in your hands sings above
the cello of the furnace, wind chimes
chattering to get in
from the cold, the lethal oboe
of wind that shakes the window
like timpani, a chamber consort
of the elements we've rightly turned
our backs on. It's warm
in the hesitant embrace
of the bird's song spinning
around us, one slim bird
that resisted the urge
to fly south. How quickly
the house fills
with its growing song.

The Satisfaction of Knowing

The Satisfaction of Knowing

"Elvis is dead," the man at the bar
says, "John Lennon gunned down
and Hemingway blew his brains
out fearing cancer, kills himself 'cause
he feared *death*, ain't that
a hoot? What I mean, though, all
the giants gone, died not young necessarily
but younger than they should have." He takes
a guzzle of beer, wipes foam
from his sensual mouth, blows his nose
in a napkin embossed with the name
of the place, the Empress of China. A comma
of suds clings to the corner of his lower lip.
"Who the hell," the fellow next to him
asks, "is Hemingway?" For a moment,
the bar is silent, the conversations
at each table and puddle having run the length
of their cycles, the silence blossoming, filling
itself with the echo of a shotgun
blast, the universe drawing a sharp breath
in surprise. "What was that?" the second guy
asks. He's pink-faced as a fresh ham, just
as blank. "What was what?" the first guy
says, turning back to the bar, to his beer,
to the satisfaction of knowing.

Old Wives' Tales

The old wives got some things right
in their tales, storks do bring
babies, their phallic bills thrusting
away beneath the soft leaves
of cabbage patches, and stitches
in time really do save
mine, yours and everybody
else's besides. Birds in the hand
are easily worth more
than any number in the bush, where
thorns conspire and black flies
are so bad, stinging out of spite
if not need. But where it counts,
they stumble on the hems
of their aprons; go on, ask them
what they think of me, of you,
of our chances.

Astrophysics

Stars fell on Alabama
with a crash, a sickening
thud, actually, and jagged
edges, tearing a hole
in the earth you could drive
a point home through
all the way to China, all
the bleeding way home. Flames
burst out of the gaping mouths
of gawkers, their eyes
kaleidoscoping backward
through time to a time
when stars were fixed points
on a blackboard sky, when things
were as you expected them
to be. The moon hit
your face like a big pizza
pie, the lazy old sun had nuttin'
to do, and Sputnik—no, they
never did warble
about that old ashcan, nothing
romantic about a half-ton heap
of nuts and bolts circling
the good green earth
every three days, like a
slow-blooming smile. But then
the sky was spinning, the earth
beneath our feet soft and porous
as tapioca, the moon
was grinning that smug smirk
that says it knows it
all, says it knows
it all, that says it
knows

After Winnipeg

After Winnipeg, Regina
seems small, sheltered,
blinkered, flat. The city
spins, hums with a motion
and sense of its own. The creek
cries out like a youngest child,
all right, I'm not a river, I am
what I am, only that, but why
do I need to be more? I pause
on the footbridge, breathing
the stink of algae, watching
for the familiar flash
of muskrat, chastened.

The Radio

In the end
he didn't have the breath
to speak, lifting
his bobbing chin
in a gesture that failed
to extend as far
as his mouth, eyelids
trembling as if to open,
as if the fading eyes
beneath them could see.

The exhausted signal
from Milwaukee wavered
in the static air, music
pulling him under
in pulses, batteries
hissing out their charge
like bicycle tires caught
on a pincushion road,
an arc of jagged lightning
illuminating the final stare,
the heat of a mouth hovering
above him, whispering
something he couldn't possibly
hear above the roar of static.

Adam's Rib

The best part of a man
is a woman, her softnesses
mocking the softness
in him, her eyes meeting
a gaze that falters, her hand
smoothing the rough padding
in his shoulder, her tongue
whispering words to the deaf.
When the tears come, as
they will, the loudest ones
will be his.

The World by the Tail

The snake was not in the grass
but the rocks by the pond. When one
of my mother's feet startled it,
it bellied across her other one, then
up her bare leg, a gaily coloured ribbon
of chalk-dry flesh—not slippery
at all, she said later, when she'd composed
herself—that paralyzed my mother, every part
of her frozen except her mouth, out of which
sprang soprano notes of the clearest quality.
"Calm yourself, Bertie," my father said,
reaching down and grabbing the snake
by its unfortunate tail and tugging, the way
you might at the end of a lawn-mower cord, flinging
it through the terrified air, a squirming rainbow.
"It's only a garter snake. He wants to be
your garter."
                        The stunned snake landed
where it should have been all along,
in the grass, and after a moment in which
it lay as paralyzed as my mother
had been, it disappeared, while my mother
collapsed into my father's arms, not in tears
but laughter. "Thank god there's no crystal
nearby," she said. "It would be in pieces."
In the pond, a snapping turtle raised
its beaked head and observed them
with curiosity. It could not know
that my sister Esther would catch it one day,
lifting it by the tail the way my father
had seized its cousin the snake. It could
not know that it would boil into soup, that
we would eat it, and a fine lunch it would be
indeed.

Bronx Cheer

The Bronx, people said, was filled
with hills and they all went up,
but I used the line in San Francisco
and Vancouver, even Colorado
where they make mountains
out of bronxhills, even down the coast
where the hills slope like cats
sleeping in the sun, their throats
rumbling with the burning of scrub.
In Saskatchewan, though, the hills
run *down*, the cold is *dry*, the wind
a perverse child that's heard
but never seen. These are the tricks
language plays, up, down,
the level playing field the newspapers
crow about all notwithstanding. The hills
we used to climb are higher now,
steeper, the path more treacherous.
Direction grows out of us, getting up
the price we pay for looking down.

The Porcupine

In the suffocating
night the porcupine
is drawn to the heat
of the highway
for breath, the hollow
of its quills filling
with an air too rich,
too cool,
for its lungs. The light
of the oncoming car
croons the swooning song
that lifts the porcupine's armour
to readiness, the trigger
of its desire poised
to set its defences
into flight, the weight
of the automobile no more
than a feather, compressed air
sighing from its tires
as the quills find their mark,
after its passage
something lying
in the road, the swallowed night
humming. The calling stars
blink out, their brilliance
punctured.

A Painting of Elvis

The night black velvet,
a painting of Elvis
in scarlet, that vivid,
that tawdry. In the middle
of the night, a flash of white,
a sob in the throat,
a perfect poem,
your beautiful ass,
rising, falling

The Dark

Forty-three years old and still afraid
of the dark, the nightlight
in the nursery more for her
than the child who slumbers
too innocent for fear. The pulse
in her daughter's temple tattoos
a message to her fingertips
across the yawning darkness,
the suffocating closeness
of the closet she has yet
to exit. *Be brave, Mommy,*
the child's blood sings.
I am with you.

Deer, Bowen Island

On the lawn below, two deer
are lying like familiar dogs, ignoring
each other and the gazes
that fall upon them. "Last year
or the year before, there were
many deformed ones," my hostess
tells me, "but this year they're
splendid." Sleek
as seals, her husband says, wiping
coffee from his silver moustache. Mist
hangs above the distant bay
like an apprehended sigh, filling
the deer with light. It is hard
to imagine, in the presence
of this health, an illness
or imperfection, mange
on a ragged rump, a two-headed fawn
born stillborn, steaming. After the coffee
has grown cold in the bottom
of our cups, Gzowski's voice buzzing
in our ears like a mother's, one of the deer
raises its head to gaze at me
with neither fear nor curiosity
nor pity. The light from within
it carves a path through the wet grass,
through the heavy air, through air
electric with singing.

Thicker Than Water

for Shaya

Blood is thicker than water
but mucus thicker still, the walls
of our guts are thick, yours
and mine, a bond between us,
the swelling in our throats no match.
Something else our bodies produce
is thicker than blood, but politeness
forbids me, a viscous ribbon
slick with disease coursing
through our systems like love
rampant in the hollow halls
of the young, pinball hormones
pinging in the archaic machines
of our bodies, fever raucous in the veins
of junkies, desire raising its head
from the ashes. Our stomachs
rumble with it, desire, this need,
this ache, our hearts
fill, empty, fill again, regurgitate,
the steady rhythm of desire
consuming itself.

On the Beach

On the beach below the boardwalk the boy
is eating ice cream, his mouth swooning
around a lush field of cold while his skin
burns, armies of soldier ants crawling
along his arm, legs, into the tender folds
of his groin, between the lids of eyes
that can see so far across water the horizon
shimmers like steel fresh from the forge, lifting
into exhausted air, fat, flatulent waves drowning
out the tinny sounds of the argument
his sister and the man in the black swimsuit
hurl off the blanket behind him like Frisbees.
The boy licks his lip, the final smear
of chocolate salty on his tongue, grit
in his teeth.
                                The hollow log into which the ants
have disappeared cannot be filled, any more
than Japan can be seen over the waves, any more
than China can be struck by digging
in the sand, the shovel and pail at his heels
just a toy, after all. The boy sniffs
the fried air, turns his head in the direction
of the boardwalk. The voices he cannot hear
have become shriller. He considers
the scent of onions, of mustard, he weighs
the sudden possibility of a hot dog.

The Rutabaga

The lowly rutabaga
is the most humble
of vegetables, the most
modest, rarely brought
to the table, considered
too crude even for crudité,
its yellow flesh pushing it
somehow beyond the pale.

It contemplates the world
of the garden from beneath
leafy brows borrowed
from its cousin the cabbage,
ruminating on the origin
of its name, *bag of roots,* testes
of the testy gardener who
first stumbled on it, his
Swedish teeth yellow with rot.

Banned from salads, the rutabaga
stews in its own juices, embittered
by the popularity of carrots,
the ubiquitousness of the potato,
always with an eye out for more. Even
the turnip, even the detestable parsnip
fares better, but the rutabaga's revenge
is sweeter, the sound of its name
rolling over the tongue with resonance
the others can only envy. Rutabaga,
rutabaga, *roooota-baaaaga, roooooooooo*
tah bay gggga. Let the potato
eat its heart out over that!

Hard Rain Falling

Forty hours, not days
but enough to wash
away the sins
of this land, you'd
think, DDT
and all its sons, teeth
still sharp in the summer
fallow. Tumescent streams
berserk in fields, lakes
vomiting pungent detritus
into basements, fungus
resplendent, triumphant,
not locusts
or ravens but a plague
just the same. God
in his wisdom has
a plan, just look
at the prune.

April Fool

Across the streaming street, a man
in tight new jeans, a better jacket
than mine and a ball cap is bent
over the dumpster intent
as any prospector, Bre-X in the news
this week, its goldfield no richer
after all than any god's half acre,
its findings salt. On the ragged lawn
so newly out of snow
the same lost flicker I've seen
all late winter at the feeder
bellies and shoulders into his work
just as intent, the red of his cap
a beacon declaring bird at work.
It happens to be April 1, but this
is no joke, men going about
their business, birds filling
their hollow bones with more
than air and desire.

At the window,
I skulk, bird watching, man
watching, wanting to disturb
neither. Later, sky dark as slate
will press down, unexpected snow
tumble to the lawn, obliterate
the trash bin, winter's last laugh
after all, but for the moment
I stand here transfixed
as the seekers I watch, poised
between hunger and flight.

Summer Solstice

in memory of Anne Szumigalski

A man with a fish tie swimming
desperately up his starched breast
is vacuuming broken glass
in the writers' room where sons
of Mennonite preachers heavy with the weight
of ancestors' anguish splinter tabletops
like metaphors caught in teeth.

The round poet squints into smoke:
"I came looking for conversation,"
she says, shaking braids that reach
without touch, "perhaps it's too late."
The earth spins silently. There is no
explanation for that which is
inexplicable, no love for those who go
beyond all reason and ken.

Outside, the endless black night
rolls into summer, a tire hissing
through tar viscous with passionate rain,
the stars tremble and skid
out of harm's way, the sky opens
like god's mouth, his tongue
tangled in the machinery of season.

The Retreat

Away for the weekend, a silent
retreat, long imagined walks
in the icy hills behind the monastery,
her head bowed in the chapel
not in prayer but thought, the endless
view from the lounge window, the valley
and the jugular vein of highway
pulsing through it below, the hard bed
too narrow to call attention
to my absence—all of this and the thing
that impresses her most
is the food, not how good it is
or how plentiful, but the way it catches
her attention. *You know how*
little interested in food I am, she reminds
me, as if I need reminding, but here
the shape of the pudding, the texture
of the lettuce in the bowl, the precise
temperature of the oatmeal on her tongue
and the size in which the beef in the stew
has been cut all engage her, as if
the preparation of meals were
a theological question, blood
of christ, blood of the lamb, *flesh*
of the lamb, the humble matzoh
all joining in debate of dietary law
with the muffled words of the brother
in shirtsleeves passing the collection plate
after lunch, as if mere food
could ever be enough
to fill her up.

Mad Cow Disease

I haven't eaten beef in years,
but now the headlines feed
my hunger, my mouth filling
with saliva, my tongue swimming
in it, drowning, my teeth aching
in absence. I long to fill myself
up with the desperation
of their cries, the solemn lowing
of the herd at evening when
the milkmaid's call settles
over the good and green land
like a lover's gesture, long
to turn myself inside out
with the peculiar demand
of disease, to feel my desire
dissolving into sponge.

Wedding Gifts

for Emily and Beth

The time you gave me a ribbon,
the time I sang for you, my heart
keeping its own ragged time
in my crystal ribs,
the time we collided in the hall
and gave each other that terrible
fright, the time the sun came up
and found us wandering around like
fools, beaming down on each other.

In our concert of years, those times
that have yet to come, the bandage
you'll kiss from my elbow, the sleep
from my eyes, the bruise on the fruit
from the corner store, the rupture
too deep to properly heal we'll tiptoe
around, the cats we'll quarrel over,
each one afraid to give in, afraid
of the consequences of winning.

Cookie crumbs in the fine lines
around your lips, laugh lines, my
finger tracing the contour. My eyes
turning down, away. Firebugs
in a bottle, the promise
of illumination, the hollow
hiss within the silence you hold
to your perfect ear, anarchy
of the heart, the quick of love.

Martin and Lewis

The enmity between
them, the loathing
and fear crystallized
as hail beating down
the shoots they set
in water, all
the laughter
trampled underfoot.

Dino died alone, just
the supermarket tabs
watching, Jerry on TV, bags
under his eyes dark
as Dino's five o'clock, poster
boys raging, biting the hand
that strokes them, 3:00 a.m.
the picture flickers

nobody laughing

Ten^2

for David and Yvonne

ten/
times ten/
times me/
times what
you said/times
that song i sang
the time you turned
your eyes away/times
this house/times the cats
their burning throats/times
ten/times the hollow in me
you fill/times everything
we could ever want/times
all we already are/
times the downy softness of
your love/times my heart
a nest/times sunlight
swelling/times
that place only
you touch/
times ten/
times me/
times
you/

the possibilities
are endless

Man in the Moon

for Catherine Hunter

Your heart is an athlete,
up at dawn doing push-ups,
stretches, aerobics to a rap beat,
running a mile before the crowds
thicken in the street, a quick shower,
then a pas de deux
with the man in the moon.

And that one?
That man never tires,
shining his stupid heart out
day and night, night and day,
singing "Claire de Lune"
at the top of his lungs
in the shower

Consider the Spider

Consider the spider,
its diligence, its meticulous
care, its hunger. Consider
the cicada, the voice
that consumes
it, consider the inchworm,
so detested yet so single-
minded. Consider
the pattern nature makes,
the design both simpler
and more complex than the poet
could ever imagine. Consider
the sun, rising and sinking
all within the compass
of just one day, consider
the moon, its pathetic imitation
somehow imbuing it
with dignity. Consider me,
consider you,
the way, against odds
and reason,
we go on.

Mothers and Daughters

Julie is going ballistic
today, berserk, screaming
her red-faced anger at the French toast
that refuses to turn, at the hunger
gnawing its way through her belly
like the rats her birth mother unleashed,
at her damaged body, at the blood
between her thighs, there for the wrong
reason, just scratches, after all.

Melanie, torn one way and the other
by these tides, fingers
the key to the empty apartment, the boom
of the silence within its walls
still rolling in her ears like waves
crashing against the dikes in Holland,
the dikes that hold the sea at bay.
She ignores her daughter because she
must, thinks of her mother
because she can not.

Alison, in her cool ashes,
is calm at last, free of pain, free
of *everything*, satisfied
to know all the imperfection
she railed against is finally
still, crystallized,
perfect, happy to know
the key is in safe hands,
her breath rising
and falling, rising
and falling

Rat-Free Province

for Yvonne Trainer

The poems she dropped
down the outhouse well
startled the rat that
shouldn't have been there,
covering it with words
like snow, like blossoms
and turning its heart
into that of a crow. Through
the other hole it flew,
through the crescent
on the door, startling the poet.
Together, they soared
to Manitoba.

Poem for a Reading in a Bar

Hey, you, you in the back,
come a little closer. The poem
is warm, but its voice is soft.

And you, you over there,
don't be afraid, the poem
bites, but only the ones it loves.

And you, yeah, I mean you,
looking so smug, do you really
think you're immune to poetry?

This poem will get under
your skin, you'll find yourself
thinking about it tonight

as you're trying to fall asleep,
your lips moving in the dark,
alone in your bed with a poem

you hardly know. When you wake
the bed will be empty, the sheets
soiled, only the poem's scent

on your pillow to let you know
it was there, only its footprints
in the snow outside your heart.

Out of Chaos, Order

Lifting its wings in Tokyo
the butterfly causes collisions
of air in Terre Haute that lifts
a sheet of onion skin from the desk
of a retired professor of ornithology,
wafting it to the open window
and fluttering it gently into the path
of a schoolboy on his way home, cheeks
red from a bully's insult, the scorn
of a girl. He kicks the paper and it lofts
again into the air, but not before
one phrase, "your darling plump breast," catches
his eye, further inflaming him, his heart
thumping in his throat as he lunges
for the paper, which floats into the naked
embrace of a tree as the boy, his heel
sliding on the wet pavement, catapults
forward onto his face, breaking
his glasses. Wet pavement? Why
is the pavement wet? Why, tears,
of course, but whose?

Latimer's Statement to the Police

Let me be clear about one thing:
I killed my daughter.
After the wife and the other kids
went to church, I put her in the half-ton,
turned on the engine, and we sat there
for a while, radio on, the C&W station
from Saskatoon, the heater rumbling
like a cat on your chest, the stars
twinkling in the sky above us
except that it was daylight and
we couldn't see them. She took my hand
and said *Daddy*, not that she could, but I knew
that's what she meant.

After a while,
I got out, told her *be right back, ain't*
I always? and went into the machine
shed, the hose right there on the bench
where I left it, a black snake in my hand
except hollow and cold, all its poison
already in my heart. It only took
a few minutes. She didn't cry,
and me neither. I stood in the barnyard
in the snow, my boots open, no gloves,
my hands cold, looking
up at those damned stars.

Radio Silence

Twins

You know how it is,
a sliver of dream
lodges itself in your head
and there it is each time
you wake, like a child left
behind at the mall, wary
of the policeman but wanting
the ice cream he offers
like benediction, like grace.
You are having a conversation
with your wife about how
to dispose of the ashes
in a sturdy ceramic urn,
the talk very everyday, practical,
and it's a while before
you realize the ashes are yours,
that you've died and been cremated,
but it was all some time ago,
the mourning's over, even you
are no longer sad, it's just
the way it is, that even-handed.

You keep waking, licking
at the dream—not all of it
but that loop, playing over
and over while you slip
back into sleep like a swimmer
in a blood-warm sea—as if it were
a thread of meat caught
between molars, too far back
to do anything about. There are
two of you, you realize, one dead
the other alive, and your wife
doesn't seem to discriminate,
each one getting her attention
in turn like two children,

the favourite, if there is one,
not likely to be shown.

In that half world
between sleep and waking
the notion doesn't seem
odd, that there should be
more than one of you, and why
stop at two? Why not dozens,
hundreds, spinning their way,
your way, that is to say,
down through centuries, peering
from the trees, glowering
through the eyepiece of armour,
squinting into the terrible
shine of war and peace, love
and the residue, the awful
aching abyss opening up
between the lives like static
electricity, waiting to jump,
the crackling, delirious snap.

But waking, you turn
on yourself, the way
a hunter will, stalking
meat too stubborn to give up
its own hunger—or is it the way
of the hunted?—walking
in your own footsteps until
even you can no longer tell
which way they point, from where
you've come. All those prints
on the ground but only one
set of feet, after all, only
one of you, staring, bewildered,
craning your neck over your shoulder
for a glimpse of reflection
of the path lying ahead.

Dec. 6, Montreal

They would be middle-aged now
the women Speck's sight blossomed
across pages, the still-sputtering
screen, nine smudged thumbprints
torn from yearbooks, the wallets
of beaux, seriously smiling,
their wounds only to be imagined,
Speck, his heart ulcered with a rage
no one, not columnists nor shrinks
pricking him with pins nor
his executioner could ever understand,
their own threads secure within
the unravelling skein. Without them,
he is no one, nothing; without him
their lives ripple on, no more
disturbed than ours.

Their names make no impression
but their faces have lost
that sheen of youth, grown
comfortable with the knowledge
of what might have been, that
nothingness that haunts them.
Mouths, noses, eyes, the cheekbones
one of them would have killed for,
the quivering lip, armed with a word.
One of them is queer, out
of the closet for years, another
thinking about it, trembling
with anger, at herself. Two are
divorced, one married again and happily,
the other alone and glad of it. One never
did marry. The others all did, still are,
are happy enough, past the stage
of trauma. They have their own lives,

they have no resentment for the death
they were spared, their lives swelled
with all the rhythms one might expect.

All still nursing except for one
who turned her back, another who went
on to med school, both of them driven
by the smell of their own blood,
the others reconciled to it,
the maddening sight of it splashed
across the sidewalk, across
their sleeping eyes, blood
filling their lungs the way
they'd all seen pneumonia patients
drowning in anticipation of return
to placental seas, that cycle
snapping at their heels
no matter which way they went.

Tonight, two of them
are working, their hands
filled with bedsores and sheets,
one is on call, staring
through the kitchen window
her eyes filled with smoke
and longing for something
she can't say, something
that won't appear in the charts,
one of them is shopping, Christmas
coming on, one is in the Philippines,
leaving footprints in sand, bloody
footprints, as it happens, her heel
gouged by a shell, two are at dinner
with husbands, their mouths full.
One is watching TV.

There is something in the faces
flashing across the bright window
that reminds her of herself, that hopeful
smile against all expectation,
that last call for dinner
in the dorm before they close
the dining-room doors, closing off
everything. The stain on the plate
where the eggs broke, spreading
their message, the stain on the floor
where she might have fallen
if things had turned out differently.

The faces scroll across the TV
like litanies of prayer, that
hopeful, that silent, that empty.
Lépine's face, though, brings
tears to her eyes, he looks
so much like her son.

The *Spreiser*

for Obie

I'm at the Y today, did
my twenty laps and I'm in
the health club, club, they call
it the club, it's a room, they got
towels, the *alte kakkers* like to sit
there after their swim, the *schvitz* room
right next door, and the phone
rings, Mendel answers it, he
listens, then his face cracks open
and he yells, loud so everyone can
hear, "A *spreiser*, this *shlemeil*
in Vancouver, he's looking for
a *spreiser*." And he turns to Golden,
"Golden, maybe you got a *spreiser*
for this *shlemeil* in Vancouver?" I should
explain, in case you think maybe
this is Jack Spreiser, the haberdasher
or Mel Spreiser, the cancer specialist.
No, a *spreiser* is a bundle
of leaves, not just any leaves, oak
the bigger the better, and tied in
a bundle just so and left to dry
six months, minimum, and then
in the *schvitz* you get it good and wet
and use it to hit yourself with, the oak
leaves, this is why it has to be oak, there's
something about them that holds
the heat. Golden shrugs. "I should
have a *spreiser*? Handle, Handle has
a *spreiser*, he knows all about
them."

and Handle
as it happens, is right next door

in the *schvitz* and Katz goes in. "Hold on,"
Mendel says into the phone, "we're
checking." Then Katz comes back, says, "Get
this gentleman in Vancouver's address."
It happens Handle
is out there in two days and he'll
bring him one. Turns out Handle makes
them himself, he's a rich guy but money
can't buy a *spreiser* the way he remembers
his own father making them and he follows
the old way, gets the leaves sent
from Quebec, puts them together
in his garage, he's got three of them
hanging there now. Ain't that
something? The guy in Vancouver
I don't know anything from but I should
tell you Mendel, Handle, Golden,
and Katz, these were all friends of
my father, whose own father had the
baths on Salter Street, a block
off Selkirk, that building's torn
down now, this is all a long
time ago, when the water in the *schvitz*
was hot.

Saving Souls

> CHICAGO—A missionary charged with killing her husband during an argument over who had saved more souls has been acquitted of murder by a judge who accepted her plea of self-defence.
>
> —Newspaper Item

I'm just a servant of the Lord,
she tells the court,
but I learned well the lessons
my husband taught me too:
riding, fixing mechanical
things that always go wrong,
aiming straight for the heart
so there would be no pain
just quick dispatch to the house
our father prepares for us all.

The argument began,
she testifies, over
housework back home
in suburban Urbana
after a lifetime
on the veldt, swept
with longing, lions
and those desperate eyes
of people wanting to learn
how to believe in something
other than themselves,
now dishes and tidying
occupied us, that
and emptying out places
previously occupied
by worthy effort.

After a lifetime
of saving souls

savings pennies
at the market
grates at the ends
of sensibilities
previously unknown,
she testifies,
that and his insistence
he'd had more success,
directed more feet
down the path leading
ultimately to salvation,
arid ground where even
love fails to take root.

When he came at me
with the raised crucifix
naturally I allowed instinct
to overpower reason
and I cowered, covering
my head like a nun, but
faith is stronger than
preservation and I remembered
my lessons well, reaching
for the staff through which
God's voice can be heard,
hoarse but distinct,
obedient to the end.

Leave Wife

> A Saudi Arabian man can divorce his wife simply by saying "I divorce you" three times.
>
> —Newspaper Item

Saying I love you three times
was enough for me, but
you wanted more, insisted
triplets of devotion
weren't enough to prove
the melding of flesh
unto flesh, the parting of
separateness, the end of two.

I told you over and over
again I troth not only
my love but my intention
and purpose, the steely
determination of a humble
man bowing to the certainty
of god's will, his blissful
interpretation of design.

But separation takes more
passion than coming
together, breaking the bond
more skill than tying it.
Words alone fade, bleed
in the points of needles
flying into one's face,
sand in a desert storm.

There's nothing I can say,
or you, to make matters
right. The law is on my
side, the law and scripture,

the heart with you. God's eye
sees more than scripture,
into the heart's own law,
where even death isn't final.

You can't say often enough,
loudly enough the words
no one wants to hear, the
terrible rending of cloth
you've worked so hard to weave,
to make a piece of. After
the words, all you really hear
is the crying out of the grain,

and we are, after all, silent
in the light of god's eye,
the terrible hollow storm
of that cry, the sudden
thrust of meaning
that goes beyond
mere words, no matter
how many times you repeat them.

Skin of Our Teeth

> Artificial human skin, being developed by a new biotechnology company, may have tremendous potential for the treatment of burn victims. The "skin" is made from cells taken from the underlayer of human skin derived from infant foreskins discarded during circumcisions.
>
> —Newspaper Item

Flesh of my flesh, blood
of my blood, this skin
I shed is no more than
Eve's own sly serpent
would offer, gladly, his
evil eye winking.

Just think, millions
of them over the years
tossed away with the *drek*,
bits of ourselves serving
no more useful purpose
within the body as without

yet now they tell us
there is balm
to be found there,
surfeit from pain,
all by the stroke
of needle and thread.

Yet if so little
can do so much, then
what if they take our
castoff hearts, oh,
not transplants, that's
not what I mean

but nurture the cells
they harbour into sheets

of something you'd
only expect to find
at the heart of god's
dominion, in his own

beating chest, tensile sheets
of flimsy, Teflony stuff
to swathe the walking wounded,
survivors of all life's ulcerating
vicissitudes, the slings
and arrows that poet talked about,

great tents of gauze
to wrap the husks of men
shelled out by all life can
throw at them, their own hearts
consumed, their bodies
riddled by acid rain

spraying from the toothy
smiles of bank tellers,
streetcar conductors, the man
at the grocer's, the woman
next door, their hands out
for their piece of heart, that

pound of flesh we wear
not on our sleeve
but just within it,
where the beating
doesn't show, the ceaseless,
effortless beating, waves

on the shore, ticking
on the mantel, the tug
at a man's groin in the heat
of passion, the peeling away
of life's sordid veneer,
exposing raw skin underneath.

Baghdad

The rain falls like sand, sharp
black rain wicking through skin
like ammonia, stinging away
fingernails left over
by the nearsighted torturer,
filling the lungs. It gets
into everything, acid water
where there should only
be dust, water in our veins,
seeping from our nipples,
polluting the semen.

After the rain, fire
falls from the dappled sky,
amorous fire insinuating
its way into our hearths, fire
without appetite that cleanses
but doesn't scald, tepid fire
that lays itself along the earth
like a mother hugging
her varied children
to her breast, consuming
them with her own need
to get under their skins,
to see herself from their eyes,
the way she really is.

At last snow falls, extinguishing
the fire with a satisfying
hiss that echoes in our ears,
builds to a crescendo,
then stutters, falling
to the rolling, gritty dunes
with the sigh of a dead man,
that quiet, that definite. We stumble

from our bunkers, dip our hands
into the icy unfamiliar, lift
it to our parched lips, the delicate
hearts burned away, the coldness
a shock finally. Each one
different, they are saying
on the radio, each one
unique, like the lives evaporated
from this scorched earth to keep
the balance of nature intact,
in order, the sacrifice we make
so abundantly of value, our blood
coagulating into ash, crystallizing
into snow, nurturing the sand.

Faith, Hope, Charity

This stage of life, there are few surprises
but pleasures enough; words never fail
to amuse me, the odd conjunctions
and twists they'll take, this evening
at the library running into a woman named
Faith I haven't seen in years, remembering
how the boys used to tease her, "Have
a little Faith, O'Malley," knowing all the while
how faithless she really was, fallen
Catholic, unreliable, railing in the regimented
way we all did those days at institutions
we were supposed to place our faith in. Later

over coffee, I was thinking of other girls
I've known whose names had played tricks
on them, poor big-eyed Hope who
hung herself, disconsolate Joy, the light
behind her eyes turned off, mean-spirited Charity
who the boys used to say of, "Too bad
she isn't named *Chastity*," awkward Grace
all feet and sharp intakes of air. I think of Robin
and Robyn, try to imagine them with worms
in their mouths, red breasts, building nests
that signal spring, think of Spring and April,
May and June, the ones I know all old women,
their names betraying them now, two aunts
called Rose, Aunt Lily, old women too,
shrivelled, closed in on themselves, the scent
of decay on their breath, Daisy
on the dock across the bay waiting beneath
the distant blinking light, always just beyond
reach. I think

about biblical names, Tamara, Michaela,
Mira, Shoshana, and Celtic names I can
barely pronounce, Siobhan tangling
between teeth and tongue. I do pronounce
the name of the woman I love,
a name I still love to say but don't say
often enough, think of the French names
that have crept into the language, Russian
names, Slavic names, the shortened names
that make girls sound like boys, the Andys
and Jackies and Stevies, the fabulous
made-up names, Ravena, Celadora, all
the names conspiring to divert attention
away from the naked lives they
conceal. It's been years

since I saw her, but I think now of a girl
I knew called Mary, her eyes wet
with nearsightedness and a fine frosting
of snow turning her hair into a halo
in the streetlight, holy night, holy
name, the names of saints whispered
under your breath like a mantra, saints
tortured for refusing to take the name
of their lord in vain, saints whose hearts
blossomed blood like the flowers
whose names they took, the names
of our mothers and sisters, the names we
call out in the dark, names we
take, finally, on faith, with grace.

Ghosts and Poets at Batoche

The rifle pits have begun to fill
in like footsteps in snow
on the crest of hill overlooking
the river bend where they cabled down
the Northcote, slicing off its hats
neat as buffalo ears, robbing it
of balance and dignity. The pits
are soft, gentle depressions in the grass
now, poke holes left by elbows
of giants tossing in night's soft mattress
beneath which those men gasped for air, antennae
rifles probing darkness, insulating
raw earthen walls with their dread.
Below the crest, down the winding stairway
summer students have put in, lies
Gunner Phillips's grave, apart from those
of his comrades and enemies, a final sentry
picketed here behind a rifle pit of iron fence,
stone marker with a puzzling date
that has us frowning as if we'd sucked
on clusters of chokecherries hanging
above the grave, their roots nourished
by calcium from Gunner Phillips's bones:
five poets and one wife arched around
the grave like mourners, singing
the old songs again.

To the east, Caron's farmhouse clings
stubbornly to blurry prairie horizon,
thrust-up evidence of gophers civilizing
the darkness below, a field that reads
flat to the eye but betrays its contours
to the approaching foot lying beyond:
the zareba, ringed by now-healed
trenches—grim fairy rings

etched in swaying grass—where
soldiers exhausted from tearing down
the house lay staring up
at the sun awaiting the attack:
this is the second house, a sign
says, rebuilt on the foundation
of the first, where "Old Jean"
and his family prospered in the years
after the rebellion had been put down
in that peculiar way the defeated—
those who survive—have of laughing
at their victors. There is no mention
of what became of them and the windows
are boarded, our vision in blocked
with the same certainty theirs out
must have been when Dumont closed
the curtain, with the same firmness
Phillips turned his eye
to the earth, to the cherry roots.
Where have they gone, one of the poets
asks, and all our minds turn
with the same precision as troopers
circling into Middleton's feint.

Outside the museum, the poem begins
to take shape. Caron's ghost appears
in the form of a young man, dark
curly hair, Gallic grin, flopping gym
shoes, and begins a conversation
with Glen, asking what he thinks
of the work that's been done, the restoration.
It's obvious he knows the site well
its history and contour, its texture
and he admits he is Caron's grandson
that his father lived in that abandoned
house, he himself in a bulldozed cottage
in the village where they mean to rebuild

now following the blueprint of the foundations
for the tourists' sake, that and history
that he was a choirboy in the church we have come
too late to see, closed for the season now.
"Yeah, I used to sing there," pointing
with his chin. We stare at him, unlaced
canvas and rubber shoes, Alberta plates
on his new Chrysler from which a boy calls
to him, "Grampa, come *on* now," and the poem
takes shape in all our heads, not the grave
of Gunner Phillips, not the tilted
farmhouse, nor the rifle pits
and trenches empty and aching as
toothaches, sky bereft of cloud, not
the dead but the living, neither
winners nor losers but survivors, neither
fear nor earth but the river, baring
its teeth, and the enduring sky.

The Immense Noise

> The age-old biological law that women's childbearing years end with menopause has fallen by the wayside with reports that specialists in "test-tube" fertilization have induced pregnancies in several post-menopausal women.
>
> —Newspaper Item

In Florida, Ponce de León following
his fine Spanish nose
found the rotten-egg spring
bubbling into promise, indigestion
spraying his face with acid
and rancour, turning
his spittle blue, an icy hand
stroking his scrotum. For this,
he forsook riches, donated
his most precious benefits,
relinquishing his own youth
in favour of the fabled.

Believe this story or not,
it strikes at the heart
of the myth the stony clerics
insist we follow that death
is only a door, swinging open
to a peace greater than any
we blinded mortals can know
in this shrivelled life,
that the cold caress
we all know on our thigh
is just an illusion,
our chattering fear irrational.

The limits that once defined
the shape of world we saw
draw farther and farther

along the horizon, the splintered sky
pushing back into itself, drawing
its own blood. The blossom bends
into the current, shaking off its own
silken coat, the thrust of its sex
naked to whatever elements develop,
dying bees bringing back a promise
of blooming late but lasting
deep into the autumn of the stalk.

If we can live forever, what else
must we be able to do, what other
invitations await in the mail
along with the flyers? Whatever
it is, we learn it at our peril
and good fortune, conquistadors
vomiting up the bloody fruit
laid out for us by inhabitants
of land we mean to steal, paradise
with a lien, a covenant
no less demanding than any other
spelled out by the stars.

Dawn. Another sleepless night.
The moving finger rattles
the ribs without pause, without
even thought, merely moving,
the sibilant hiss blotted up
by the immense noise bubbling
from the heart,
the age-old law crumbling
against the onslaught
of desire, of need, the lines
of the crumpled road map running
into each other.

Fathers

after Leesa Streifler's Lament

In your dreams, your father
is wearing duckbills, false
moustaches to amuse the girls
fluttering through your parties,
his eyes copper coins throwing
their reflections back at them,
his image pulsing in black
and white, wavering
in the acidy bath, materializing
before your eyes. My father
liked to say "duck-bill platypuses,"
the collision of syllables
amusing him, "duck-billed
plat-a-pus-essss," and
"pet'r-o-dac-tyl," the sounds
rolling off his tongue with
all the certainty of specific
knowledge, "the funniest creature
in creation except for you,"
he would say, his finger
quicksilver in my side, our
laughter disturbing
the air. In your dream, duck-billed
platitudes fill the background
space, flat-footed explanations
attaching themselves in clusters
to open hearts, bees
at the wounds of flowers.

Within the frame, the dazed duckling
vague as breath, vague as an idea
still taking shape, forms beside the egg-
head of the man wearing a duckbill
like a sword, like a phallus, some

thing to stand between him
and the object of his lies, growing
longer with every sigh. It's too
simple to say the man is
your father, that the shaft
of his proboscis—a Jimmy Durante
word my father liked—is pointing
in the direction of your future,
any more so than that my father
lies behind the words I write, his
finger still goading me on.
There are times, you at your canvas,
I at the page, we have to loose
ourselves from ghosts
riding our shoulders through
the night, echoes still whispering
in our ears, the drone of bees
mumbling goodbye.

That Summer

In the barn where we played
the beams would creak with the weight
of the body of the boy who hung
himself there fifteen years before, sunlight
slanting in through gaps in the rafters
on blackened bales of straw sour
with rot. The boy had stood
on a pile of bales, Clay said, tied
the rough hemp noose around
his neck, said a final prayer, and kicked
his way into eternity. We laughed
at the thought, and Clay made
a face, his head tilted crazily, tongue
protruding, a sound like what we all
imagined a death rattle would be
splitting his lips. *When they found him*
he had a bone-on the size
of a baseball bat, Clay said, and we all
grew silent contemplating
the irreducible paradox of death
lined with the force and thrust
of life, the kicking legs growing
still, the throat silent, and still
the body defiant.

Ten, eleven, twelve,
that's all we were, Kenny and me,
Clay and his brother Tim out
from the city for the summer
at their grandma's, the farm one over
from Schaefer's, just this side
of the abandoned one with the haunted barn.
There were copperheads by the broken dam,
sleek and lethal as lightning strikes, and the one
we thought we'd killed rustled and raised

its head in the raft, striking at Clay, who
pissed himself before Kenny brought the axe
down so hard we had to abandon ship,
laughing so hard we almost pissed ourselves
too, Tim waving the snake's body, already
going dull, at his brother. Years later,
Kenny and I heard Tim broke his neck
when the jalopy he was driving spun out
at 120 and Clay, who hadn't given a damn
about anything, bought the farm in 'Nam
when he stepped on a booby trap, snakes' tongues
of steel pincushioning his body. Ain't that
something? Kenny said. But they weren't pals
of ours, so it didn't really matter.

Radio Silence

> Police and observatories have been swamped with calls about a mysterious light in the sky in recent days, but there's nothing to worry about, a scientist said today. It's not a UFO but the planet Venus, which is at its closest point to Earth in years.
>
> —Newspaper Item

Above the belching whir of silence,
evidence of some distant intelligence
crackles, the universe flexing
its muscles in preparation for response
to a question not yet posed. The light

spitting in our eyes may be no more
than reflection of our own purpose,
signals of a resolve not yet reaching
a certain resolution. Better to blink
than allow the retina to be violated

by energy without thought. *Venus!* Goddess
of love, flicking her flashlight through
god's backyard, picking her careful way
across the cool mossy stones of the path
to the glider, her reckless heart filled

with the *chirrup* of satiny frogs
in the celestial pond, calling their own
hearts out. Afraid to make a sound, afraid
someone may be listening, afraid someone
isn't listening, afraid of what she

might have to say if someone is, if
someone calls her name. *Hush.* A finger
to her lips, she contemplates the blue-green
world spinning above her, gasses thick
as lamb's wool emitted from its glossy seas,

burbles of steamy violence telegraphing
from the antennae it projects toward her
and all her sisters, on all sides. No,
better to keep her own counsel, silence
in answer to this calculated indifference,

better to say nothing when the answers
are so obvious, the solution so finite,
definite, easily defined. Better just
to shine, to let her light precede her,
heaven's smile radiating before its teeth,

before the clamour, the rush of silence.

Twenty-Fifth Reunion

this is the first day
not of the rest of my life
but of the look back,
the autobiography,
the autograph of the person
i was, worm inside the cocoon
that became the butterfly i am,
automatic as the sun's blinking
away god's green grass's night tears,
autoerotic as me seeing you
in the mirror.

since i left you much
has happened, but it was
so long ago it broils
in the memory like chalk
shivering time's backbone:
endless, thoughtless sky
of iowa, the snowball fights
in colorado, california's
pink rain, the steady hum
of railroad tracks lifting
their breasts to the new jersey central:
folded in between the postcards
a life slivers, sharp edges
to catch fingers on, draw blood.

always, the moving finger writes
its way through dust's sheen
etching history the way
a quick-sketch artist at the fair
captures the moment in time
you occupy, war and peace, canada
and the rattle of typewriter
keys, the hiss of paper, lilacs

squeezing the last breath of colour
out of evening, the final scent
wafting its way to a heaven closer
than you realized.

this is what it amounts to
then, autonomous lives
swept away by design, autocracy
ruling the path from school
to blankness to college
to stupidity to university
to stupor to army, marriage, job
and around again, the way we came
in, the way it goes around, love
tiptoeing its way through
the shrapnel, the falling stars
a disinterested sky exhales, signs
god cares, his autograph, my
signature, luminous, telling
my own story.

Community

Three in the morning, there's no place
lonelier than the Safeway lot, its ragged carts
lined up under the fluttering phosphorous
like children at a Romanian orphanage,
jagged as teeth grinning in the open mouth
of a sleeping drunk, the community sleeping
not like a drunk, not like a baby
but like a drunken baby, its face
blurred with grease paint, its fists curled
in an innocence they haven't thought
of yet at the bagel shop, the bakery
or the tea room, leering at each other
through windows heavy with sleep.

Tonight, Cathedral is sleeping, its head
in the creek, feet on the tracks, both arms
stretched into jumbled traffic, a worried frown
creasing its smooth face as it tosses
and turns. It worries about tomorrow, about
who will clean the litter from its streets,
strip the graffitied posters from the walls,
write the words we've been expecting,
the words in the letter from home, the home
we've left and cannot return to, the absence
at the centre of the page. Instead, we look
across the street to our neighbours,
the blustery people with the barking dog,
the teenagers and the midnight stereo.
The scent of their cabbage rises
into the air like the perfume of lilacs
about to burst into flame
all across the neighbourhood.

In her sleep, one child curls and uncurls
her hand like a damp flower, her face
still red as a bruise from the parade.
It is Paul's child or Brenda's, or Bruce's.
She is dreaming of the fair tomorrow,
the dragon she will be, the tub of water
the pitch will douse her in. She is dreaming
of the woman she will be, the boy
who will haunt her, his muffled car
parked beneath the broken light
in the Safeway lot. She is dreaming
of shopping carts, the empty ones
that grin at her, their teeth filled with seeds,
the full ones that bring her home to the house
on the corner with the cats and the broken
fence, her arms filled with promise.
She is dreaming,
though she doesn't know it,
of community.

Barium Moon

For two days he fasted.
Eighty-five years old and his bowels
had shut down, no complaints, just
refused to work. Appetite, sure
and no pains above or below
where the belt would be if he still
wore one, relying instead
on suspenders, the way, he was
pretty sure, Dief had in his later,
not better days. No, no pains,
not even discomfort except
for a bloated feeling that drove
him as often as once an hour
to the throne, resplendent
with *Reader's Digest*s, which had,
he couldn't help cracking to the doctor,
better digestion than he. All that
commotion for nothing. The boys
in the back room on strike.

Now, two days of consommé and Jell-O,
his teeth aching with absence and
making him think for the first time
in years of Dick Gregory, the comedian
who had stopped being funny, whose
hunger had driven him to swallow
himself. Tomorrow
he would swallow the barium with
a dramatic flourish, remind the tech
how Socrates had refused to turn away
from the hemlock, no taste too bitter,
ever, and let them chart the road map
his intestines made in their winding
way to the ocean, yeah, that was it,
behind their lead aprons they'd be

cartographers, brave Kelseys awash
in unexplored seas. No, he was mixing up
the metaphors, he knew that, smiling
at his own improbability.

He had
plenty of time to think about it
the last evening, the final dose
of foul ropy liquid washed down
with the umpteenth glass of water,
his gullet so afloat, it seemed, he
had to force the last drops down, like
a drunk unwilling to waste
the dregs of blood-warm beer turning
to stain against the glass. That had
done it, the cork blowing and every
foul thought, deed, and desire coming
back to haunt him now, streaming
out of him the way curses do
from the mouths of street kids, just
as dirty and thoughtless but at
the other end. The bathroom
reeked with him, his thighs wet, heart
alive as a bird alert to the presence
of cat, his mouth—this the odd part,
what with all the water he'd sucked
up—parched. The torrents of spring
coursing through him as if he were
merely the channel, it was the life,
his own life reduced to so much flotsam
and jetsam, and that was putting it
politely.

Sprawled out on the stinking
floor, he could see the fleshy slice
of moon tangled in the naked arms
of poplar outside the bathroom

window. It reminded him of a time—
oh, back a century or two ago when he was
just a slip of a lad of seventy-five—and he
happened to glimpse a leering moon
from the window of a streetcar,
exclaiming out loud enough to raise
the chin of the respectable *baba* sitting
in front of him. "The moon,"
he'd told her, "I haven't seen it
for ten years or more." Not seen
the moon? Well, not really, not with
all the scar tissue over his eyes,
transplanted from his heart. Now
the moon shone in his eyes, a candle,
a flashlight, headlights of an
oncoming car, a bullet, making
him turn away, making him gasp, then
cry out in fright.

Was this the way
he would die? His life down the toilet
not as a metaphor, jumbled or not, but
real as the crack in the lino his thumb
was caressing? Full of shit all his
days, now squeezed dry, empty as a can
of lard the pigs have been at, rooting
for themselves. Coming and going,
coming and going, the tide
washing upstream into the benign mouth
of that pumping channel, purifying it
with salt. Might as well open a vein
and really do the trick, let everything
out, the obscene moon licking its runny
lips over the twisted husk of a man
it gets just a glimpse of, peering
through the window. *Chaff!*

For a long time
it is the sound of that final thought
ringing in his ears like a mantra
that sustains him. But nature has her
witty ways. He hadn't thought there was
any more, could be, but she calls,
a gurgle of gas with his name
pressed to its lips like those
of a lover, rushing from him
like wind through trees, leaves
quaking with delicious fright. "Goddamn
if I'm not alive," he says,
his voice so feeble it wouldn't scare
the roaches if there were any. "Full
of it as ever." Yes. And hungry, damn it.
Famished. Greedy, he gorges himself
on the moon.

A Warm February

Long before the cancer that killed her
began its malevolent stroll through
her body, its appetite growing,
my mother began to emit a scent,
a not-altogether unpleasant perfume
that I only realized after her death
was its foreshadowing, a butler
announcing the arrival of lord
and lady so-and-so at a fancy dress
ball. This was a bathroom smell,
a smell that came from deep within
her, nothing that deodorant
could hide or showers wash
away. It clung to her skin, in her hair
like the smell of tobacco and port
on my father's fingers, like coffee
in a kitchen long after the cups
and pot have been washed and put
away.

When she fell ill, we had to travel
a long way through air too thin
to breathe, the sight of her gasping
for breath outside my window, flickering
above the wing. We landed in a February
that had forgotten how to be winter,
its breath warm as a puppy's, smelling
of milk, and rode a bus interminably
through darkness blacker than any
I could remember, starless, moonless,
long stretches of highway with neither
streetlight nor beckoning windows
of passing houses, signs of intelligence
on a distant planet suddenly

brought home, the whole night holding
its breath.

My father was late
arriving at the hotel to pick us up,
unused to driving at night, he'd taken
the predictable wrong turn coming
into the town he'd shopped at
for twenty years, his excuses clumsy
as his outstretched hand, a muffled
kiss on the top of her head for my wife,
who took the wheel, navigating us safely
to a home she had never lived in, my father
beside her pointing out the new
sights, a new development on the Dilts corner,
this old fellow, the farmer with the apple trees,
dead, the son of this couple runaway, gone, my cheeks
burning, the sight of the battered mailbox
at the corner, my parents' name, my own name
stencilled in fading letters, squeezing
my heart.

The dogs, rough and unkempt, butted
their heads against our knees as we piled
out of the car into a silence broken only
by their sighs, the night so warm the cicadas
should have been singing, the air
should have been thick with the fragrance
of lilacs, of roses, the delicate pink
kind my mother loved
so much, planted like hedges all
around the house, their thorns
no protection, after all.

We didn't garage
the car: tomorrow, we would drive
back into the city, envelop ourselves

in that scent whose origin I would
gradually come to know, a perfume
distinct and recognizable as the earth
beginning to thaw. But for now,
while my wife buries her head
in the redolent fur of the dogs,
my father and I are stranded
in the porch, inexplicably colder
than outside.

"It's the bad thing,
isn't it?" he asks, unable to say
the word, he who can speak
two languages, laboriously read
five, who taught himself Latin and Greek
and French so he could read Caesar
and Homer and my mother's love
letters, unable to say one simple word.
I turn on the light so as to better observe
this, but he flicks if off again so I can't see
his face. All around us, the warm darkness
butts at our legs and we embrace
to keep from falling, hold each other
in the enormous, hollow night. Perhaps
that *is* cicadas I hear.

DAVE MARGOSHES is the author of the novel *I'm Frankie Sterne,* the novella *We Who Seek: A Love Story,* four collections of short stories, and two previous volumes of poetry (*Northwest Passage* and *Walking at Brighton*). He has won a number of poetry awards, including the Stephen Leacock Poetry Award in 1996. Margoshes's stories and poems have been published in dozens of magazines and in numerous anthologies. He lives in Regina, Saskatchewan.